REAR AREA
SECURITY IN RUSSIA

REAR AREA SECURITY IN RUSSIA

The Soviet Second Front Behind the German Lines

PREFACE

This pamphlet was prepared by a committee of former German generals and general staff officers under the supervision of the Historical Division, EUCOM, in the early part of 1948. All contributors had extensive experience on the eastern front during the period 1941–45. The principal author, for example, was successively G4 of an infantry division and assistant G4 of a panzer army in Russia.

The reader is reminded that publications in the GERMAN REPORT SERIES were written by Germans from the German point of view. As in DA Pamphlet 20–230, *Russian Combat Methods in World War II*, and DA Pamphlet No. 20–231, *Combat in Russian Forests and Swamps*, the "Introduction" and "Conclusions" to this study present the views of the German author without interpretation by American personnel. Minor changes in form and in section titles have been made to secure greater clarity, and tactical examples have been rearranged to illustrate better the growth of the partisan front between 1942 and 1944. However, passages which reflect the author's prejudices and defects, whatever they may be, have not been changed and find the same expression in the following translation as they do in the original German.

CONTENTS

		Page
Section I.	INTRODUCTION	1
II.	GERMAN PLANS AND PREPARATIONS	4
III.	THE FRONT BEHIND THE FRONT	13
	1. Interference by Isolated Russian Units	13
	2. German Attempts to Restore the Local Economy	15
	3. The Rise of the Partisan Front	19
	4. Attacks on Rail Communications	24
	5. Disruptions of Highway Traffic	30
	6. Attacks on Supply Depots	32
IV.	CONCLUSIONS	34
	MAPS	
	1. Reference Map ....(facing)	40
	2. Railroad Demolitions ....(facing)	40

This pamphlet supersedes MS No. T-19, "Rear Area Security in Russia," published by the Office of the Chief of Military History, Special Staff, U. S. Army, in July 1950.

SECTION I

INTRODUCTION

This study on the problems of rear area security is based on German experiences during the Russian campaign. Particularly striking examples have been selected which show most clearly the type of disturbances created by the Russians, the German countermeasures taken against them, and the lessons learned from experience. The same, similar, or different circumstances were encountered in other theaters of war. Accordingly, a variety of security measures became necessary and many new experiences were gathered. Yet, the fundamental questions remain the same everywhere.

Seen from the Russian point of view the problem might be stated as follows: "By what means or methods can I most effectively cut the lifeline of the enemy's fighting forces, either for a short time, or, if possible, for an extended period; where can I disrupt the line in such a manner that the effect will be felt at the front?" The answer is a definite combat method which has the typical characteristics of a blockade. It can be executed with relatively small forces and limited means; by allowing for the mobilization of the populace it represents a morale factor as well as an increase in fighting strength, while offering further advantages through the use of sabotage and espionage behind the enemy lines.

A country as vast as Russia, where many sparsely settled areas offer an abundance of shelter and concealment, naturally provides much greater possibilities for the use of this combat method than countries with different terrain. An additional factor is the strong natural inclination of the Slavs toward fighting from ambush and under cover of darkness.

From the German point of view, the problem might be approached in the following manner: "What active and passive measures of security must be employed in order to deprive such combat methods of their effectiveness or to reduce their effect to virtual insignificance?" Such considerations should not be confined to purely military aspects. In varying degree the politician, the public administrator, the military commander, and even the ordinary soldier have to deal with these questions. Uniformity in understanding and in meeting the problem, from the highest to the lowest echelon, is a fundamental prerequisite for success. Furthermore, one should never be caught unawares by combat methods of that type. By careful advance study, not only of the country itself but also of the people, their customs, cares, and needs, as well as their hopes and desires, one must be prepared to meet such methods and even to anticipate new tactics on the basis of current experiences.

It should be emphasized at this point that whoever makes use of this combat method constantly gains new experience which will enable him to improve and intensify his actions. Different methods are developed from day to day, and some of them are likely to be fundamentally new. The tremendous technical advance of the last 10 years has placed entirely new and undreamed-of means of great effectiveness at the disposal of mankind. Even if one disregards the practical application of atomic energy, rocket weapons alone constitute a substantial element of destruction. Further possibilities may lie in the harnessing of nature's own functions. Just as science has recently succeeded in producing man-made rain, it is conceivable that a way might be found of causing a coating of ice to form on switch tower installations, turntables, and switches, so that railroad traffic may be temporarily paralyzed. At the height of battle such measures could be of decisive importance in hampering strategic troop movements, as well as transportation of fuel and ammunition. It would be profitable, therefore, to employ at an early stage the most capable experts in technology, physics, and chemistry who are able to apply, as well as to counteract, such modern methods of warfare. This is one field where no limit is set to man's imagination. At any rate, to be prepared means to save lives and to limit the range of those incalculable factors which must be expected in any war.

It is a fact supported by many examples in military history that events and conditions behind the front lines have often failed to receive sufficient attention. In all but a few cases this has worked to the disadvantage of the front. Combat forces, while they are in contact with the enemy, should never have to concern themselves with security problems of areas that lie behind them. That should always be the responsibility of higher echelons.

Rear area communications are comparable to the blood vessels of the human body. The most capable brain, the strongest arm, the most powerful heart can no longer fully perform its functions if the blood cannot follow its prescribed course through the vital arteries. It was with these ideas in mind that the following study was prepared.

During the Russian campaign, the most significant and instructive examples presented themselves in the area of Army Group Center.

From the wealth of material available for this study, primarily based on the personal recollections of the contributors who had taken part in the Russian campaign, only those examples were selected which had been duplicated by experiences on other sectors of the front. To that extent the present report may be considered generally applicable.

The areas of Army Group South (Ukraine) and Army Group North (Baltic States) were not favorable to partisan activities. Reasons for this are to be found in the well-known political conditions. Army Group Center, however, entered old Russian territory at the very outset of operations.

SECTION II

GERMAN PLANS AND PREPARATIONS

When the first plans were laid for the campaign against Russia, the problem of security for all the necessary supply routes through the vast areas of the future theater of operations played a significant part. In the light of historical experience, a considerably greater enemy effort against the German supply lines was to be expected than in previous campaigns with their relatively short lines of communications, or in any of the areas already occupied. But the main point in all deliberations and the primary factor in all phases of military preparation was the vast expanse of Russian territory. Obviously, all supply routes would have to be considerably longer than ever before and thus more susceptible to incursions of all kinds. This was true not only for all roads, rail lines, and waterways, but also for all points at which supplies were to be stored. Anyone aware of these facts could virtually anticipate the location and number of probable danger points and the strength of the forces required to eliminate these security threats.

Deliberations over the type and extent of essential security measures led to the conclusion that, in this field also, a new approach had to be found. No longer was the main danger focussed on the same areas as in previous campaigns, for the operations zone of an army now appeared to be much less exposed than the areas farther to the rear. Areas in close proximity to the front are always the scene of strong concentrations of forces which have firm control over the local rail and road net and are in a position to keep the local population under close surveillance. In such areas it was, therefore, possible to maintain constant supervision and a high degree of security without employing a large force exclusively for that purpose. Any special security forces that were saved in this manner could be used to better advantage in other areas where the danger was greater, while those remaining in the combat zone could now be assigned to more specific tasks.

An entirely different situation prevailed in the rear areas where the vastness of the country, sparsely covered by German troops, presented a constant problem. Here, in view of the over-all manpower situation, only a limited number of widely dispersed occupation units could be employed. The constant lengthening of communication lines because of the rapid progress of operations produced an increasing need for security forces, a need that was even greater in the rear than in the vicinity of the front lines. These considerations determined all

German plans for the protection of communication lines, a factor of vital importance to the outcome of the entire operation.

From the outset a distinction was made between *active* and *passive* security measures. For the purpose of active security, special units of various types and strength were created. At first they were organized in the form of separate battalions, and only in those instances where unusually extensive installations had to be protected were several battalions combined under the control of a security regiment headquarters. Most of their personnel was taken from older age groups and consisted largely of veterans of World War I or of men who had received a minimum of training in replacement units. They were led by older reserve officers or retired officers who had been recalled to active duty. These facts need to be emphasized for the better understanding of the difficulties which these units had to overcome later on in the performance of their tasks. Nevertheless, many of these security units gave an excellent account of themselves, particularly when the growing manpower shortage necessitated their employment as combat troops at the front.

They had a variety of weapons in altogether insufficient quantities. When the Replacement Army was no longer able to furnish an adequate supply of small arms, which were then more urgently needed at the front, the security units had to be equipped with captured Russian weapons. It is quite obvious that units outfitted in that manner and often inadequately acquainted with their new and unfamiliar weapons were extremely limited in their usefulness, except for areas where little or no trouble on the part of the populace was to be expected.

The unusual extent of all prospective operations in the East prompted the German High Command to lay plans for the establishment of a security organization that would be more or less independent of the armies operating in the forward areas. For this reason the area immediately to the rear of an army group operations zone was designated as an army group rear area (*Rueckwaertiges Heeresgebiet*). There, using his own forces, the army group rear area commander was to be responsible for all active security measures, for the pacification of enemy territory, and, consequently, for the protection of all lines of communication. Whereas in previous campaigns no more than weak security units had been organized and employed, the arrangement for the Russian campaign included the formation of entire security divisions, largely similar in composition and equipment to standard infantry divisions, but subject to certain variations depending on the availability of personnel and matériel. These units eventually proved capable of conducting an active defense against enemy forces appearing in army group rear areas. The areas assigned to individual security divisions varied in size from 5,000 to 10,000 square miles.

The security and pacification of occupied enemy territory behind the army group rear areas was to be the responsibility of the military occupation authorities, an arrangement that had fully proved itself during other campaigns. Their administrative agencies were to cover the occupied territory in a network of *Kommandanturen* [administrative area headquarters] of various levels, such as *Oberfeldkommandanturen* [divisional level], *Feldkommandanturen* [regimental level,] and *Ortskommandanturen* [company level]. Security forces of various strengths, as mentioned above, were to be assigned to these administrative units, depending on the size of the areas to be controlled. During the course of the Russian campaign, this organization made a substantial contribution toward the maintenance and security of German lines of communication from the homeland to the front.

Perhaps it should be emphasized at this point that to assure the security of future supply routes, active precautionary measures must be taken, even during the advance, to prevent the destruction of vulnerable objectives. This is especially true of the main supply carrier—the railroads.

On 22 June 1941, for instance, during the very first hour of the Russian campaign many road and railroad bridges were saved from destruction by the swift and surprising action of a few small combat patrols. Later these bridges were of invaluable importance to the entire German supply system in the East and in some instances actually provided the basis for further successful operations. During the course of the entire war, many objectives of vital importance to the transportation of supplies, such as bridges, underpasses, viaducts, railroad shops, and water supply installations were secured intact because of the energetic action of advance detachments. This was of particular significance in the case of railroad bridges which, if destroyed, would have required a long time to be restored to normal operation.

In the final analysis it was the master plan of the Chief of Supply and Administration which determined, more than anything else, the over-all structure of the security organization. Although recognized as a primary prerequisite, the immediate availability of the railroads as a carrier of supply could not be expected and, at first, was not taken into account. It was assumed that the roadbeds would be unusuable because of demolitions, that the Russians would remove all their rolling stock, that the difference in gauge would necessitate the re-laying of tracks, and that considerable partisan activity would be encountered. Therefore, all German plans for the movement of supplies were initially based on the use of the sparse road net that existed in Russian territory.

Armored spearheads were to be accompanied by heavy motor truck transportation units carrying supplies up to a distance of about 300 miles from the base. In this plan the supply of the more slowly advancing infantry divisions, which were equipped with horse-drawn vehicles, was also taken into consideration. The motortruck transportation units were to establish supply depots approximately 50–75 miles apart. These installations were to be set up in the immediate vicinity of large communities and preferably close to favorable railroad facilities. Particular emphasis was placed on the establishment of safe and adequate facilities for the storing of large quantities of supplies. As the combat elements continued to advance, a special security force was to be assigned to each of these supply depots to assure their undisturbed organization and improvement. The strength of these forces depended on the size of the installation, the area that had to be guarded, and the degree of danger from partisan activities. Generally, the plan called for a regimental headquarters with the usual number of security battalions in the case of a larger town, while a battalion headquarters with the corresponding number of smaller units was to be employed for the protection of smaller installations. As far as possible, front line troops were to be relieved of all such security assignments. As it turned out later, this policy could never be fully enforced.

The protection of these supply depots involved a variety of problems. Internal security consisted of guarding the supply dumps and adjacent buildings and facilities. Since these installations were to include warehouses for *all* classes of supply, as for instance rations, clothing, ammunition, fuel, medical and veterinary equipment, as well as motor vehicles and spare parts, the need for security forces grew considerably as operations progressed. This circumstance had to be taken into account in all planning and especially in organizing security units. Furthermore, all installations necessary for the maintenance and operation of the supply depots, such as power plants, railroad stations, and airfields, as well as the billets of the security troops themselves, required additional protective measures. The mere fact that some of the larger supply installations might well assume the proportions of a medium-sized city may offer an indication as to the number of security troops that would become necessary.

The supply plan called for each newly installed supply depot to organize a forward echelon which was to move up behind the combat forces along the most suitable road. At these central supply depots, other smaller supply depots were to be organized and distributed laterally in both directions. In this manner the infantry divisions, regardless of their route of advance, could obtain their supplies without the necessity for long-distance hauls. A "block system" of successive guard posts was to be established to safeguard the flow of supply from one depot to the next.

In addition to the forces required for the above-mentioned tasks, security troops were to be furnished to the several armies to protect their base supply depots and installations and to relieve the combat forces as soon as possible of all security duties. Experience had taught that the actual combat elements were excessively burdened with such duties and thus often deprived of forces which were urgently needed at the front.

The initially established supply depots were to remain in operation until the Russian railroads could be converted to normal gauge and the supply bases advanced into the zone of operations. Then, as supply depots farther to the rear would be dissolved, their security forces could be made available for employment in forward installations. Another possibility for the release of security troops on an even larger scale would arise as soon as a previous zone of operations or an area under military control was taken over by a civilian administration. The police forces of this administration were then to assume the former duties of the security troops.

According to the original plan, the initial requirements of security forces were to be met by selecting combat units that had proved themselves during previous campaigns. Subsequent needs had to be covered by organizing new units. It was clear to all concerned that this plan would never produce a fully satisfactory result, partly because of the vastness of the prospective theater of operations and partly because of the limited replacement potential, which would certainly preclude the large-scale organization of units for purposes of security only. This view was later borne out in practice. To an ever increasing degree transportation and supply units of many types, and frequently even front line troops, had to be charged with the above-mentioned duties.

German plans for active security also called for an active air defense. Antiaircraft artillery units were to be provided for the protection of large or particularly important railroad stations, workshops, bridges, and similar installations. In each case the strength of these units depended on the availability of personnel and the importance of the installation. They were to be under the control of regional air force commanders.

Fuel trains and similar shipments, which at a later stage of the campaign became unusually valuable, were to be protected wherever possible by railroad antiaircraft batteries consisting of 20-mm. four-barreled guns mounted on flatcars. These units were under the command of the army group rail transportation officer.

Since it was quite obvious that both manpower and matériel for security purposes would be limited, special consideration was given to the problem of *passive* defense. Thorough training of all agencies and forces concerned with the moving and handling of supply was recognized as a primary prerequisite for passive security measures. The combat troops themselves can contribute in many ways to the security and preservation of scarce and valuable supplies, and thus increase their own readiness for action as well as their combat efficiency. Combat and service troops alike received continuous instruction by appropriate directives and orders and were further trained by means of demonstrations and field exercises.

Of the many *passive* means of protection, the following may be mentioned: Over poor roads, through endangered areas, or at night long supply columns were to move quickly and without interruption; single vehicles were to avoid passing through partisan-infested areas; full use was to be made of the block system of security established along the roads by driving in convoy from block to block; and unloaded supplies were to be dispersed for protection against destruction from the air.

Particularly after 1943, as a result of experiences gathered during enemy air raids, unloaded supplies of all classes were generally placed underground. Only in this manner was it possible to preserve large quantities of supplies, which up to that time had been prize targets for the Russian air force. Protection for ammunition of all types was assured not only by means of dispersal but also by storage in tunnels and bunkers. In the case of fires caused by bombing attacks this method of storing had the obvious advantage that the spreading blaze caused considerably less damage to ammunition dumps than on previous occasions.

The precious motor fuels were stored in trenches protected by banks of earth on both sides. Drainage ditches were dug which, in the event of a large fire, would allow the fuel to flow off quickly and thus diminish the danger of an expanding blaze. The storing of rations required a greater expenditure of material and labor, especially in the case of valuable food supplies which had to be protected against spoilage due to moisture.

The passive air defense of railroad lines, buildings, and other railroad installations was carried out at the request of, and in close cooperation with, the regional transportation agencies. In army areas this was the responsibility of the local commanders, in army group rear areas that of the rear area commanders. Security forces of the type discussed in the earlier part of this study, particularly security divisions, were employed for this purpose. In areas where additional protection was required because of heavy partisan activities or the presence of important railroad lines, these security forces were at times supported by other German units that happened to be in the area, such as combat divisions which had been withdrawn from the front. As a last resort, the so-called emergency alert units were called upon which, though formed specifically for this purpose, were not too highly valued. In areas under the control of civilian occupation authorities, all security functions mentioned above were assigned to the regular police forces.

On many occasions, replacement transfer battalions and casual detachments en route had to be employed in the defense of endangered railroad lines. The trains themselves were protected by so-called transport security regiments. They were subordinate to the army group rail transportation officers and received their specific assignments from regional transportation headquarters. Troop transports and personnel on leave trains were responsible for their own security. For the protection of freight trains, cars were attached which offered observation and fields of fire over the entire length of the train.

Railroad lines and installations were protected by a system of block control points and by security patrols operating along the lines. In wooded areas both sides of the tracks were cleared to a width of 300 yards to prevent partisans from approaching without being discovered. Among the many protective measures developed during the course of the campaign the following might be mentioned at this point: One or more flatcars loaded with rocks were used in front of particularly important trains to provide protection against pressure and vibration-type mines. In some instances a whole train of empties was placed ahead of the train that was to be protected. Mobile construction units were distributed along the railroad lines. Amply equipped with construction materials and interconnected by a telephone circuit, they could be immediately directed to any point where the railroad had been damaged by enemy interference. At a later stage, when telephone poles became a favorite object of destruction for the partisans, demolition charges were inserted which would detonate if an attempt was made to cut or fell the poles. An item of civilian railroad equipment—a special mine-clearance device without crew—was placed in front of the trains to set off enemy mines in the roadbed by subjecting the tracks to continuous vibrations.

In the operation of the railroads, various protective measures were introduced. They included travel at low speed (at night not over 10 miles per hour); movement of several trains in convoy; rerouting of trains insofar as the lines permitted; and placing the locomotive in the center of the train in order to protect it from immediate destruction in case of mine explosions. Later on, when large numbers of Russian railroad personnel were employed, particular emphasis was placed on their closest surveillance.

Specific measures of passive air defense—a matter of paramount importance for railroad stations and junctions—comprised the transfer of all central switchboards from railroad stations to the outside, so as to create individual loop circuits. In the construction of new installations considerable intervals were maintained between buildings. As soon as they were occupied, all vital installations and all personnel quarters were immediately protected by every available means against the effect of bombs or fragments. Troops were frequently quartered in trains which were taken out onto open track at night.

In close cooperation with the supply agencies the unloading of all shipments was to be accomplished in the shortest possible time. As a standing operating procedure at night or during air raid alerts, all railroad stations were to be cleared of trains carrying ammunition and fuel. If supply trains could not be unloaded promptly, they were to be separated and their individual sections distributed as far as possible over all available spur tracks.

The aircraft warning service of units in the area was hooked up with the railway signal communication system, so that all traffic control agencies could be alerted in time and with maximum speed. If the wire lines were destroyed, these warnings were to be transmitted by radio.

As the above-mentioned plans and precautions indicate, the German Army High Command was by no means caught unawares by the strong partisan activities encountered during the Russian campaign. It was known for some time that the Russians were determined to use organized partisan warfare in the defense of their country and that they had used propaganda to spread the idea among their population. Their future military leaders in partisan warfare had been carefully trained in the use of this combat method. Just before the start of the campaign—according to information received in Germany—the Russian War Academy conducted war games in an area where certain locations were designated as so-called partisan centers.

Similarly, the Russian High Command had recognized at an early stage that, in contrast to the dense railroad and highway networks of the highly urbanized West with its ever-present possibilities for alternate routes, the very few serviceable supply routes through the vast expanse of the Russian area were of paramount strategic importance. Furthermore, in view of the great distances, the poor condition of the highways (which easily deteriorated under the influence of the weather), and the anticipated shortage of motor vehicles and fuel on the German side, the Russians realized that the main burden of supply would have to be carried by the railroads and that this would be equally true of all large-scale troop movements, furlough transportation, and evacuations. Clearly cognizant of this handicap, which would present itself in any military campaign against Russia, the enemy began early in the war to build up a "second front" behind the German lines.

SECTION III

THE FRONT BEHIND THE FRONT

1. Interference by Isolated Russian Units

During the first 6 months of the Russian campaign, the German supply system generally functioned without major interruptions. Either the enemy had failed to recover from the initial blow, or he was yet unable to muster the proper means for effective raids on German rear communications. Isolated attacks were made on German supply units, and at times entire divisions were cut off from their supply base for a short period. But actually this was always the work of organic Russian troop units or of groups of stragglers who, in their attempt to fight their way back to the east and rejoin their own forces, had to cross highways or side roads and on such occasions came into sudden and unexpected contact with German supply units. In these engagements, the supply troops were mostly at a disadvantage since they were hardly prepared to meet a fully armed opponent. At the very beginning of the Russian campaign the drivers of supply trucks, for instance, were inadequately equipped with small arms, and machine guns were lacking altogether.

In the fall of 1941, a heavy truck transportation company was proceeding along the Slutsk–Bobruysk road. The convoy consisted of 30 trucks with trailers and a crew of about 75 men. Because of excessive dust an interval of 50 yards was maintained between vehicles, which were moving at a speed of about 15 miles per hour.

When the leading truck rounded a curve, a large Russian cavalry force suddenly came into sight at a distance of about 1,200 yards—apparently in process of crossing the road from south to north. At the same time the truck column drew fire from the front; what appeared to be an antitank shell went through the windshield of the leading vehicle and into the cargo without injuring anyone.

The truck stopped at once; its crew, with the exception of the driver, jumped off and took up positions about 25 yards ahead. An antitank gun was spotted in a ditch about 300 yards down the road. The company commander, who because of the breakdown of his own vehicle, had been riding on the leading truck, ordered his men to open fire on the Russian gun crew. Meanwhile the assistant drivers of the other vehicles had been brought up and placed in position. A motorcycle messenger was dispatched to notify the military commander of Slutsk and request assistance.

By now the enemy was also using machine guns and his volume of fire increased steadily. On the German side two machine guns and 30 rifles had been brought into action. Soon the first casualties were caused by the very accurate fire of the Russian antitank gun.

To save the vehicles, which were loaded with ammunition, the company commander ordered the drivers to take their trucks about 1 mile back on the same road and to wait out of sight with their engines running. Great skill was required to turn the 20-ton trailer trucks around on the narrow road. Screened by clouds of smoke billowing from the leading truck which had been set on fire, this maneuver succeeded. About an hour later the company commander received word that the order had been carried out.

After another hour and a half reinforcements came up from the rear and went into position. Finally, elements of a machine gun battalion arrived on the scene and its commander took charge of the fighting. The men of the truck company could now be withdrawn. Their losses amounted to one dead and seven wounded, with three ammunition trucks and trailers destroyed. Subsequent reconnaissance and interrogation of prisoners established that the truck company had run into elements of a 2,500-man Russian cavalry unit which had crossed the road on its way into the forest area south of Minsk.

The company had accomplished its general mission of protecting its cargo and of keeping it from falling into the enemy's hands. Had the convoy not been carrying ammunition, the outcome of a prolonged fire fight with an enemy of the described strength would have been extremely doubtful. Certainly the 30 rounds of ammunition which each man carried on his person would have proved inadequate. It was only because of the nature of the supplies loaded on the trucks that the enemy could be held at bay until reinforcements arrived.

At the time mentioned, the local inhabitants were generally cooperative everywhere. They welcomed the German forces as their liberators and desired nothing more fervently than to resume their normal, peaceful activities. This attitude was demonstrated in many ways. It was a common occurrence for mayors to request protection against scattered Russian soldiers who had formed bands in the deep forests and conducted raids against German troops and local inhabitants alike, primarily for the purpose of obtaining food, civilian clothing, and other necessities. Frequently, German supply units or delayed single vehicles had to bivouac in deep forests and passed the night without suffering any damage. On some occasions the local inhabitants actually warned German troops against bands operating in the vicinity and called their attention to specific danger spots.

2. German Attempts to Restore the Local Economy

The German combat forces, at least during the initial period of the campaign, made every effort to restore normal conditions in the areas they occupied and to gain the confidence of the local population.

In the summer of 1941, the eastward advance of a German infantry corps was halted temporarily by strong resistance near Rogachev in the area of Bobruysk. At the same time a supply bottleneck had developed which made it necessary to fall back on supplies that could be obtained from the surrounding territory. For the purpose of administration and local management the corps area, insofar as it was not affected by the fighting, was divided into subareas and placed under the control of the divisions. The area assigned to one particular division covered about 40 square miles and extended between the Bobruysk-Roslavl highway and the Berezina River.

Under the control of the division's supply and administration echelon the area was subdivided into districts similar to those of the former civilian administration. Each district was under the management of an officer or a civilian official of the division to whom a permanent interpreter was assigned. These officers and officials were relieved of all other duties and had to be present in their districts at all times. They were instructed to take up personal contact with the people, particularly with the older and more influential inhabitants, and to make every effort to gain their confidence.

Even in peacetime the area around Bobruysk had figured in the war plans of the Soviet High Command as a potential center of organized partisan resistance. As early as 1940—as the Germans found out later—the Russian War Academy had made this area the scene of special partisan war games under the direction of General Kulik who was yet to play an important role in actual partisan warfare. It was all the more remarkable that only 1 year later, because of their judicious handling of the population, the Germans were able to keep the inhabitants at peace and, moreover, to utilize the resources of the region for their own purposes.

When the area was first occupied, its peacetime economy appeared completely paralyzed. The bulk of its agricultural and industrial machinery had been either destroyed or removed by the Soviets. In keeping with the Russian mentality, all work in the cities was at a standstill and the fields lay fallow. Everybody seemed to be waiting for a direct order to start the wheels turning. As a first step in that direction all existing enterprises were seized and inventoried under the supervision of the district officers. Then all plants that were still adequately equipped received orders to resume operation immediately. In other cases attempts were made to replace damaged machines or missing matériel.

Russian mayors and collective farm managers were charged with the responsibility for getting the work in the fields under way, and soon the first harvests were brought in. Next, the grist mills, dairies, bakeries, and workshops of local craftsmen were put back into operation. Salvaged tractors, with fuel for them, were issued to the local civilian agencies. Egg collecting points, grain depots, and milk delivery stations were established. The marmalade factory at Bobruysk resumed operation under the direction of one of the division's disbursing officials who happened to have previous professional experience in this particular field. While the plant provided employment for many Russian laborers, both male and female, its products were welcomed by German troops and local inhabitants alike. All financial transactions were left entirely to the Russian civilian agencies, subject only to final supervision by German experts. No friction of any kind resulted from this procedure.

To assure the proper treatment of the Russian population, all German officers and noncommissioned officers appointed to these administrative posts were given a short orientation course by German experts on Russia. The redistribution of collective property was begun with the greatest caution, so as to cause the least possible disturbance to the general structure of the local economy. Collective workshops were abolished and henceforth every craftsman was permitted to practice his trade freely. For the repair and rehabilitation of factories and for their subsequent operation, skilled laborers were placed under the supervision of men with suitable background who were drawn from the German forces or even from the native population. The administration of state farms (*Sovkhoz*) was decentralized, and they were turned into local agricultural cooperatives.

Thus the division was soon able to cover at least part of its supply needs from local sources without actually robbing the country, while making a notable contribution toward the improvement of the overall supply situation. Within a short time a variety of articles was produced in the area under the division's administration. In addition to foodstuffs and similar items, the products included horseshoes, hardware made by local blacksmiths, and tow ropes for the horse-drawn units, especially for the divisional artillery. The local inhabitants were immediately reimbursed for all deliveries by certificates of value received, and the amounts were credited by the Russian local administration against their requirements of every-day commodities.

It was not without significance for the establishment of good will among the inhabitants of the area that one of the division's chaplains happened to be a native of Russia who had a good command of the language and was fully familiar with the Russian mentality. With the arrival of the German forces all churches had been reopened everywhere, and German troops and local inhabitants met in common worship. The news spread rapidly throughout the area; from afar Russian parents would bring their children to Bobruysk to have them baptized by the German minister in the newly opened church.

Once a feeling of mutual confidence had developed, the dance- and music-loving inhabitants arranged village festivals at harvest time which were regularly attended by German district officials and members of the security units.

Any arbitrary acts by German troops, such as the unwarranted slaughtering of cattle, plunder in any form, or the wanton destruction of property, were most severely punished. This served to protect the few possessions which the Soviet regime had left in the hands of private individuals and strengthened the confidence of the people in the fairness and justice of the German forces. For some time after August 1941, when it had to resume its advance toward the east, the division remained in touch with the area that had been under its control until increasing distance made all further contact impossible.

With the arrival of the occupation forces, which assumed control over the Bobruysk area following the departure of the German combat division, the picture changed from the very outset; the population was treated in a manner quite different from that to which it had been accustomed. Whereas previously certain regulations pertaining to freedom of movement in the area, curfew, etc., had been somewhat relaxed, they were now rigidly enforced. Every rule of common sense was suddenly replaced by strict adherence to the letter of the law. Such methods naturally had the effect of lessening the confidence of the people in the good will of the occupying forces. Particularly the well-meaning elements among the population, who had demonstrated their willingness to cooperate fully, were now sadly disappointed, whereas their opponents rejoiced and hastened to exploit the new situation for the benefit of the partisans and their counterpropaganda.

Eventually the new occupation forces proved incapable of taking effective measures against the partisans, who were now operating under the command of Marshal Kulik. The Germans gradually lost control over the entire area around Bobruysk, which became one of the most dangerous centers of partisan activities. German rear communications were continuously disrupted, while troop movements, railroad trains, and truck transports were harassed by persistent attacks.

The preceding example may serve as an illustration—even though on a limited scale—of the many advantages to be gained by the pacification of occupied territory, provided of course that forces are employed who are properly trained and adequately prepared for their task. This was not an isolated incident. Other German combat units were even more successful in enlisting the active cooperation of local administrative officials.

In the fall of 1941, a German division advancing toward Bryansk encountered heavy enemy resistance in the area of Pochep and had to assume the defensive on a broad front. As a result, the divisional supply point was located for some time at or near Mglin (20 miles northeast of Unecha). Here also, following the successful example of Bobruysk, a Germany military headquarters was established for the purpose of administrative supervision and area management, while the local Russian administration was reconstituted and staffed with new personnel.

In numerous meetings with the town council, arrangements were made for the resumption of work in local crafts and trades, as well as for the assurance of an adequate food supply. Soon the harvest was under way; then grist mills and distributing agencies resumed operation. It was even possible to reopen a print shop and a tannery which served the German forces, as well as the local inhabitants. With the aid of the Russian mayor, who was extremely active and willing to cooperate, a program was initiated for the repair of damaged housing and the construction of new dwellings. Offenses against the occupying forces were handled by German military courts with the cooperation and advice of local experts. In no instance was it necessary to inflict the death penalty or to take hostages.

In the town of Mglin and throughout the surrounding area peaceful conditions were soon established. Without disturbance the inhabitants continued to pursue their normal occupations. It was increasingly evident that after a short period, during which the activities of the German troops had been under careful scrutiny, the occupying forces had succeeded in gaining the confidence of the people. The same reaction was found even among the large Jewish population living both in the town and in the rural districts. During that entire time the front lines were no more than about 25 miles away. In all other respects the pacification of the area was accomplished in about the same manner as described in the preceding example.

When the division finally had to leave, it also tried to maintain contact with the region that had been under its control. But here again the same administrative blunders turned an initial success into failure. The occupation forces which took over proved incapable of protecting the population against the partisans, and quickly destroyed all confidence by their unreasonable treatment of local inhabitants. The police forces assigned to the area soon began to recruit forced labor and to persecute the Jewish elements of the population. Six months later this area also had developed into a hotbed of partisan activities through which supply transports were routed only in extreme emergencies.

3. The Rise of the Partisan Front

By late fall of 1941, occasional acts of sabotage by groups and individuals had become routine. The beginnings of a well-planned partisan organization that operated with a variety of technical and psychological means were clearly noticeable. A typical Russian institution based on national tradition, this organization grew steadily in size and importance throughout the entire war.*

There can be little doubt that by the winter of 1941–42 the basic pattern of the Soviet partisan organization had been established. To lay the groundwork in German-occupied territory, Russian agents under the guise of helpless civilians took advantage of the kindheartedness of the German soldier by passing through the lines and infiltrating to the army group rear areas. Other agents who had been left behind during the retreat of the Red Army gradually began their work. Many of them were women who felt that they could count on protection by the German soldiers.

Changes in the attitude of the population soon gave evidence of the incessant activity of thoroughly trained agents who made the best of apparent weaknesses of their German opponents. The people were told that the inevitable return of the Red Army would be a day of reckoning for all those who had collaborated with the occupying power. On the other hand, strong appeals were made to their national sentiment. "Shame and death to those who collaborate with the enemy! Save Mother Russia!" was a typical slogan. With great skill, the Russian propagandists exploited every mistake made by the occupying power in the treatment of the local population. Eventually these mistakes, more than anything else, served to undermine the initial confidence of the people in the Germans and in German propaganda.

Whereas the local inhabitants up to that time had been friendly, trustful, and entirely willing to cooperate, their attitude changed greatly during that first winter. While they did not commit any overt acts, they clearly displayed more restraint in their relations with the

---

*Ed.: See also DA Pamphlet 20–230, *Russian Combat Methods in World War II*, pp. 108 ff.

German occupying forces. Many of them took great pains to avoid being seen during daytime in the company of German soldiers. It became more and more difficult to find men who were willing to accept local administrative posts. Here also the terror tactics employed by Soviet agents began to make themselves felt.

The next step was the formation of small bands which established their hideouts in the forests. They forced the inhabitants of the area to supply them with food and give support in other ways. At first their activity was confined to more or less coordinated raids on targets of opportunity. They attacked smaller German camps or supply depots, raided and plundered single vehicles on the road, blew up Russian industrial enterprises that worked for the German troops, and took with them any Russians who were working for the occupying power. Occasionally, they carried out demolitions of railroad lines which could often be repaired without major delay in operation. In some instances even German railway construction units working under insufficient protection were attacked and wiped out by partisan bands.

Early in 1942, in order to facilitate the movement of supply through difficult terrain or partisan infested areas, attempts were made by the German forces to restore some of the railroad lines that led into the corps sectors of the Second Panzer Army. Individual railway construction units were employed which had to provide their own security as they advanced along the tracks to make the necessary repairs.

In this manner, a railway construction company was assigned to the Bryansk—Dudorovsky sector, about 50 miles east of Bryansk. Strictly on its own the company worked for weeks on one particular section of the track. Eventually several days passed without any report being received from the unit. Investigations revealed that the entire company had been wiped out by partisans while it was working near Zhurinichi (15 miles east of Bryansk). All repairs on the section were immediately halted, and the line was of no further use since no additional forces could be spared to strengthen the security of the construction troops. The search for the partisans who had carried out the raid proved fruitless. Thereafter, to prevent the recurrence of such surprise attacks, railway construction units were no longer sent out alone unless they could maintain daily direct contact with nearby supply depots or combat troops.

By 1942 Russian partisan warfare against the German rear communications had entered a more advanced stage. A network of channels for transmitting orders, thoroughly planned in peacetime, reached from a central headquarters in unoccupied Russian territory up to the western border of Russia and, in some regions, even into Polish territory. Whereas prior to that time individual messengers, crossing the lines in the guise of harmless civilians, had sufficed to maintain communications and transmit orders, this task was now regularly performed by courier planes and even transport aircraft. These airplanes forwarded instructions to the partisan groups operating behind the German lines and supplied them with arms, ammunition, signal communications equipment, motor fuel, medical supplies and other necessities. They always carried full radio equipment to maintain contact with each other and their central headquarters.

That these flights were very numerous could be established by German ground and air observation; abandoned parachutes which were often found by German reconnaissance patrols offered very definite indications. Apparently the partisan planes operated only at night; they landed on well-concealed air strips deep in the swamps and forests or dropped their loads over temporary drop zones identified by light markers. Partisan headquarters, air strips, and drop zones were perfectly protected by natural cover and impassable terrain obstacles. Although numerous radio messages emanating from partisan centers could be intercepted, it was impossible to establish the accurate location of their transmitters and to take effective countermeasures either on the ground or from the air.

In the fall of 1942, a German army operating southwest of Orel was ordered to assure the delivery of a certain quota of grain and potatoes from the local harvest. Agricultural control officers (*Landwirtschaftsfuehrer*) were posted throughout the entire army area to supervise and direct the harvest operations carried out by the local inhabitants. Equipped only with small arms and scattered widely to include even the smallest villages in the area, these agricultural control posts could not be expected to offer effective resistance in the event of partisan raids. The harvest had no sooner been brought in when reports about increased partisan activities began to mount. Numerous partisan raids on harvest control points had the result of frustrating gradually the entire agricultural program until the German control organization was virtually driven out of all harvest areas.

Thus, in the absence of adequate security forces, which could not be spared anywhere else, the Germans gradually lost control over an area of great agricultural value. Local inhabitants reported that the partisans were continuously seizing and carrying off grain supplies. Other accounts indicated that Russian airplanes were landing every other night in the partisan-held forests around Bryansk, supposedly to pick up the grain seized by the partisans and to transport it to the east. These reports could actually be verified by German reconnaissance which observed landing lights in various places. But since these air strips were obviously located in areas held by strong partisan units, any interference from the outside was impossible.

In this manner the Russians succeeded in exploiting an enemy-occupied area to the advantage of their own war effort, while the Germans, ostensibly the occupying power, were unable to take effective countermeasures. Thereafter, whenever German troop movements or antipartisan actions were carried out, they were also used as an opportunity for salvaging and removing local stores of all kinds.

In February 1942 a Russian plane shot down in the Orel sector was found to carry a recently completed moving picture film on the "Russian Counteroffensive Against the Invaders, Begun on 6 December 1941." The film was obviously intended to be shown in the rear areas in order to bolster the morale of the partisan groups and the local population. On their return flights from partisan areas such aircraft usually carried messages and reports, captured weapons, and wounded partisans. Occasionally, they even took along important German prisoners, as in the case of Brigadier General Max Ilgen who was captured in the German rear area and flown to Moscow during the same night.

Generally, the following may be said about the origin, type, and size of Russian bands operating behind the German lines: Organized partisan activity usually began with the formation of small, isolated bands of from 5 to 20 members who were hiding out somewhere in the woods. Even during the gradual buildup of the entire partisan organization, these basic units remained fairly independent. Their activity was initially confined to raids of opportunity conducted for no other purpose than to supply them with booty. What held them together was a certain spirit of adventure, probably a natural trait peculiar to many of their members. It did not take long until the over-all partisan organization extended also to bands of that type. They were fitted into a well co-ordinated plan and were employed chiefly to harass certain areas. In addition, larger groups were organized, some of which reached a membership of several hundred. Constituted along military lines and led and employed as military units, these bands differed only in their appearance from regular Russian combat troops. Most of their leaders were well-trained professional soldiers, some of them even general staff officers. They were brought in by parachute or glider or, wherever possible, were landed on partisan airfields. Most partisan groups were equipped with small arms and heavy weapons; a few even used artillery which the Germans had captured and then abandoned for lack of suitable transportation facilities after the encirclement battles of the first weeks of the war. On many occasions large bodies of Russian combat troops were separated from their main force and sought refuge in the dense forests. There they were organized into partisan groups and employed in operations against the German lines of communication.

In the spring of 1943 the Second Panzer Army, comprising about 35 divisions, was engaged in defensive operations in the Orel-Bryansk area. The main burden of supply was carried by the double-track railroad line Gomel-Unecha-Bryansk-Orel, which at the same time had to transport part of the supply for the adjoining Second Army in the Kursk area. A single-track railroad through Krichev-Surazh, which joined the main line at Unecha, was available for occasional use and provided some relief. Another single-track line from Smolensk through Roslavl to Bryansk served as an additional supply route. Motor transportation depended primarily on the main Smolensk-Roslavl-Bryansk highway. The road leading up from Gomel via Unecha, because of its exceedingly poor condition, was used only in emergencies. Moreover, it crossed some of the worst partisan areas and for that reason was bypassed whenever possible.

Strong partisan bands were located in the forests west of Lokot (south of Bryansk). They had been formed of Russian soldiers, cut off in the Vyazma-Bryansk encirclement battle, who now received their instructions from partisan headquarters somewhere in unoccupied Russian territory. Particularly during the Russian breakthrough into the Kursk area in the winter of 1942–43, they constituted a serious menace to the deep flank and the rear of the Second Panzer Army. In order to provide protection against these bands the Germans employed native units recruited in the area around Lokot. After the above-mentioned encirclement battle numerous Russian stragglers also were left in the forests around Kletnya and Akulichi west of Bryansk. Large sawmills located in that area were soon taken over by the partisans and, according to reports, some of the lumber was even transported to Moscow by air. The bands established in these forests conducted persistent raids on the road and railroad line leading to Roslavl. Thus the German communication lines into the so-called Orel salient were exposed to partisan attacks from all sides; the unpleasant consequences were soon to be felt in all supply operations of the Second Panzer Army.

The following security forces were available to the Second Panzer Army for defense against partisan bands and protection of German lines of communications: one security division to protect communication lines running north and southwest of Bryansk and to conduct antipartisan operations in the forests north and northwest of the city and in the area around Kletnya; several security battalions to guard the depots in the vicinity of Bryansk and to protect the road and railroad line to Orel, as well as the connecting roads in the area of Zhisdra; and native Russian formations to provide security around the town of Trubchevsk (south of Bryansk). These native security units had been formed for the primary purpose of protecting the local population against marauding bands of scattered Russian soldiers. From their hideouts in the forests, these bands made daily forage raids on the villages in the open country and subjected them to ruthless pillaging and plundering. The local inhabitants, therefore, had braved the dangerous woods to gather abandoned weapons, ammunition, and equipment for their own use against such attacks.

All the security forces mentioned above were engaged day and night in antipartisan activities. They guarded the depots, bridges, and other vital installations. They furnished security detachments for the protection of trains that had to pass through endangered areas. On the roads they manned the control points established for security purposes and escorted the columns of supply trucks from one point to the next. In view of the large number of partisan bands and the vastness of the partisan-infested areas, it is not surprising that these security units fell far short of accomplishing all their tasks. According to reports by local inhabitants, it was in these forests that bands of White Russians had held out until 1926 or 1927 without ever being captured by the Soviet Government.

The partisans replenished their ranks in several ways. They brought in replacements from the unoccupied part of Russia; in their own areas they used the regular Russian conscription system to draft able-bodied individuals who were then trained in partisan units. Some of the bands acquired a high degree of mobility with the help of abandoned or captured German motor vehicles or by using sleighs and skis in the wintertime. Once a partisan band was known to operate in a certain area, one never knew just where or when it would strike next. That close liaison existed between the Russian leaders *behind* and *in front of* the German lines was clearly noticeable. Immediately before and during Russian offensives partisan bands were concentrated at strategic points, and their activities increased to the scale of major operations.

4. Attacks on Rail Communications

Throughout the Russian campaign the railroads remained the chief carrier of supply. German logisticians had hoped that the lines would be available and had constantly emphasized their vital importance to all operations in the East. But nobody had counted on so early an operation of the railroads as was actually possible in the course of the campaign. What this meant to all German movements was clearly recognized during the first muddy season in the fall of 1941, as well as during the winter that followed. Without the railroads all German supply operations would simply have come to a standstill. German motor vehicles, exposed to excessive wear and tear over roads in poor condition, were deteriorating rapidly, so that a considerable proportion of the motor tonnage was soon unavailable for the movement of supplies.

The enemy did not take long to recognize his advantage; the number of railroad demolitions through partisan action increased steadily. The methods employed varied with the purpose the enemy wanted to accomplish. Daily interruptions of traffic were caused by rail demolitions for which the Russians used various types of mines.* Pressure- and vibration-type mines were placed in the track, to be detonated by the locomotives. To destroy particularly valuable supplies, such as gasoline in tank cars, the partisans used mines with pull-type fuzes which were set off by remote control. Retreating Russian forces often buried mines with long-delay fuzes, under the tracks where they might blow up as much as 3 months later. Mines with simple delay-type fuzes were also employed to avoid hitting the previously mentioned protective cars ahead of the locomotive. In order to escape the mine detectors, nearly all of these mines were placed in wooden containers, and their construction was of the most primitive type; some of them consisted of no more than a small package of explosives with a safety fuze. Occasionally, even magnetic mines were used. They served as means of sabotage in workshops and on standing trains and were mostly equipped with delay-type fuzes.

In the fall of 1943 four supply trains were destroyed simultaneously at the Osipovichi railroad station, and all traffic on that line had to be suspended for a long time. Investigations revealed that a magnetic mine had been attached, presumably by a native railroad worker, to one of the tank cars of a gasoline train. When the mine went off it set the car on fire, and the spreading blaze soon enveloped the entire train. An ammunition train standing nearby was ignited and blew sky high, setting fire in turn to an adjacent forage train. Finally, a fourth train loaded with "Tiger" tanks suffered the same fate and also burned out completely. The shortage of personnel as well as the lack of extra locomotives made it impossible to save even part of the trains by removing individual cars. Moreover, the explosion of the ammuni-

---

*Ed: See also DA Pamphlet No. 20-230, *Russian Combat Methods in World War II*, pp. 60ff.

tion train had caused considerable damage to many of the switches, so that the line itself was no longer in operating condition.

Similar disruptions were caused when locomotives were fired upon with antitank rifles or bazookas. In addition, various acts of sabotage were committed by Russian railroad personnel who, for lack of German manpower, had to be employed in large numbers to keep the railroads in operation. About 110,000 Russian railroad men were used in the sector of Army Group Center alone.

At a later stage, demolitions were frequently combined with raids on disabled trains, which resulted in even greater losses of rolling stock and longer delays in the restoration of the lines. An excerpt from the monthly report of the Chief of Transportation, Army Group Center, covering the period from 1 to 31 August 1943, contained the following information:

"Despite the employment of special alert units for the protection of the railroad lines, partisan activity increased by 25 percent during August 1943 and reached a record of 1,392 incidents as compared with 1,114 for July. The daily average amounted to 45 demolitions. In 364 cases the rails were cut simultaneously in more than ten places. Individual demolition points amounted to 20,505, while 4,528 mines could be removed. During the night from 2 to 3 August the partisans began to put into effect a program of large-scale destruction. Numerous demolitions were carried out which caused a serious curtailment of all railroad traffic and a considerable loss of railroad matériel. Within two nights the six to seven thousand miles of track in the area were cut in 8,422 places, while another 2,478 mines were detected and removed prior to exploding. Several lines could not be put back into operation for a considerable time.

"Another major handicap in the operation of the railroads was the increasing number of sabotage acts, committed chiefly by native workers under partisan orders. These acts resulted chiefly in a severe shortage of locomotives. In many instances, the so-called eastern volunteer units (native formations) which were employed to protect the railroad lines made common cause with the partisans and took German weapons along with them. In one case, for instance, an entire Russian security detachment of 600 men went over to the partisans. On 17 August 1943 this force attacked the Krulevshchizna railroad station. Using the machine guns, mortars, and antitank guns which they had taken with them at the time of their desertion, the Russians caused considerable damage. German losses in that engagement amounted to 240 dead and 491 wounded. Altogether, partisan activities from 1 to 31 August 1943 resulted in damage to 266 locomotives and 1,373 railroad cars; about 160 miles of track were rendered unserviceable." (Map 2.)

The operation of the railroads was often seriously impaired when their own signal communication lines were cut. This was usually done by sawing off or felling individual line poles. As a rule, such minor acts of sabotage were hardly the work of partisans but rather of otherwise harmless civilians who were acting under the pressure of Soviet agents.

With time the partisans developed a definite system in the disruption of railroad traffic. In support of major operations, for example, they were no longer satisfied with destroying the lines at certain points but carried out mass demolitions with the effect of disabling long sections of the track. Partisan operations on the ground were often combined with attacks from the air directed primarily against railroad stations, rail junctions, bridges, and particularly important railroad lines. Such actions, as previously mentioned, were carefully co-ordinated and usually indicated that the enemy intended to launch an attack against the German lines.

Until the fall of 1942 Russian air activity against German supply lines was confined to isolated attacks which did not appear to follow any definite pattern. There were occasional bombings of railroad stations, supply dumps, or roads, but these raids did not cause major disruptions or traffic jams. The situation remained virtually the same during the winter of 1942–43. But a radical change came with the spring of 1943 when the German forces began their strategic concentration for an offensive south of Orel (operation ZITADELLE).

At first the main railheads at Orel and Bryansk were blasted day after day by the Russian air force. The loss of supplies and railroad matériel was felt immediately, since the lines were now not only serving the Second Panzer Army but also bringing up supplies in preparation for operation ZITADELLE. At Orel a supply train loaded with one million rations received a direct hit and went up in flames. As the fire spread, it destroyed an army ration dump which had not yet been dispersed and placed into underground shelters.

At the eastern edge of Bryansk, bombs were dropped on an ammunition dump which resulted in the loss of about 1,200 tons of ammunition. The Bryansk railroad station was hit repeatedly at the peak of its night traffic. In contrast to the usual procedure the station had to be kept in operation at night because of the heavy load carried by the feeder lines. On one of these occasions a train loaded with ammunition for the Second Panzer Army was blown up, and the fire spread to another train carrying the equipment of a division in transit. Consequently, the entire reserve supply of arms and equipage of that division was destroyed. As another ammunition train was leaving the station, the last few cars were hit by bombs and the train was set on fire.

As a countermeasure, all army supply dumps in the area were immediately separated into smaller dumps. This could only be accomplished by using all temporarily available motor transportation, chiefly, corps and division vehicles, with the added disadvantage that now even more security forces were required than before. Moreover, the new dumps were no longer close to good railroad facilities. This in turn, tied down an excessive number of vehicles and caused the consumption of more gasoline. Wherever possible, supply trains were broken up before reaching the unloading stations and rerouted by individual carloads to those corps which had their own railroad facilities. The railroad stations were completely cleared of all cars by nightfall. Another countermeasure was the unloading of supply trains somewhere along the line, just prior to reaching the last damaged section of the track. At such points the supplies were transferred directly to organic army vehicles or even to trucks of the front-line units proper. But this again was a measure which required additional personnel, tied up a large number of trucks, and caused a substantial increase in the consumption of gasoline. Therefore, it was soon necessary to reroute supply shipments over the Roslavl-Bryansk line, which became the next major target for Russian air attacks.

The Seshchinskaya railroad station, 55 miles northwest of Bryansk, was completely destroyed by heavy, successive bombing raids. In that area the highway ran close to the railroad line, and the temporary destruction of both made it extremely difficult to bring up the men and matériel required for repairs. For some time supply trains were taken only as far as Roslavl, and from there all supplies had to be carried forward by army group trucks. All available repair units were now placed along the main railroad line in order to restore it as quickly as possible to full operating capacity. They succeeded for short periods of time, and soon individual supply trains could be pushed through as far as Bryansk or at least to a point outside of Pochep where the supplies could be transferred to motortrucks.

When the enemy realized that he could not bring about the complete isolation of the Orel salient by air attacks alone, he tried to disrupt the German lines by ground tactics. In a series of demolitions, the partisans cut the main railroad line as far back as Gomel. In this situation again the close cooperation between the partisans *behind* and the enemy forces *in front of* the German lines, with all its detrimental effects upon the German supply situation, became clearly noticeable. As a last resort, some of the trains were now diverted over the single-track Krichev-Unecha line. In the absence of any reserve forces, there was no way of strengthening the security of roads or railroad lines. But in spite of all obstacles and difficulties, the Germans managed time and again to get a lone supply train through to Bryansk.

Meanwhile, the offensive plans of the Russian forces facing the front and the flanks of the German salient had become apparent. On the German side the need for supplies became even greater than before. Corps and divisions had to use every imaginable expedient in replenishing their dwindling supply from army dumps.

In March 1943, the main supply line into the Orel salient was completely interrupted for some time. The break occurred about 15 miles southwest of Bryansk where a double-span railroad bridge crossed the Desna river. The paramount importance of this bridge had been impressed upon the commander of the rear area, and he had been repeatedly warned that the structure was to be protected and kept intact at all costs. The commander had therefore assigned a security platoon with antitank weapons to the task of guarding the bridge. One of the German reliefs which failed to take the proper precautions and was observed by the enemy from the neighboring woods, fell victim to a partisan night attack. The leader of the covering force had neglected to assign his men before nightfall to their individual defensive positions. At the crack of dawn the partisans first made a feint assault from the west. Once they had succeeded in distracting the attention of the security unit, a group of 200 to 300 men attacked the bridge from the east; the guards were overrun and the bridge blown up. The main line was now blocked to all traffic.

All available railway engineer and maintenance forces were immediately put to work to deal with this emergency. They constructed crib piers of railroad ties which had to rise to a height of 60 feet. It took 5 days before the improvised structure was usable for single freight cars, and these had to be moved across by hand. After little more than a week the bridge was capable of supporting entire trains without their locomotives. Each train had to be pushed on to the bridge from one side and pulled off from the other.

During the same night in which the bridge was destroyed, other partisan forces disabled the relief line running from Krichev to Unecha by cutting it in 90 places over a total length of about 60 miles. As a result, both lines were out of operation at the same time.

During the night of 19-20 June 1944 the partisans carried out a major operation in the area of Army Group Center. This was 1 day prior to the Russian general offensive which eventually led to the collapse of the German Army Group. Altogether, the partisans attempted 15,000 demolitions on the railroad lines running through the area and were successful in 10,500 cases, all in the course of 1 night. Their main effort was directed against the supply lines that served the Third Panzer Army, the same German unit which was to bear the brunt of the first heavy attack by the Red Army on the following day.

As an immediate result, *all* double-track lines were blocked for a period of 24 hours, while the operation of single-track lines was interrupted for over 48 hours. This was another example that demonstrated the excellent coordination between the Russian combat forces and partisan headquarters behind the German lines. Obviously, the sudden collapse of its entire rail transportation system had disastrous effects upon the operations of an army group engaged in a desperate struggle at the front. It was too late to apply effective countermeasures, and only a few temporary expedients could be found to relieve the situation.

5. Disruptions of Highway Traffic

The undue burden on the railroad net, coupled with a widespread lack of efficient railroad lines, forced dependence on highway transportation for a substantial part of all supply shipments. As a result, the roads soon became favorite targets of partisan raids. This was especially true for stretches leading through dense and extensive forests, where the partisans found perfect concealment and could not be pursued by German troops. The tactics employed in these raids followed generally the same pattern: A German motor convoy traveling through a dense forest would suddenly run into a log barrier constructed at a blind spot on the road and, while coming to a halt or trying to turn, would be exposed to devastating enemy fire from all sides. If any vehicle managed to escape to the rear, it was only to be caught and destroyed in another road block set up by the partisans in the meantime.

Cutting of telephone lines was another means of paralyzing road traffic. It always called for a time-consuming and painstaking effort on the part of the line crews who had to find and repair the breaks.

The partisans frequently laid mines on the roads. Without causing any serious damage this had the effect, at least, of blocking traffic for short periods of time. Virtually all of these mines were no more than wooden boxes of primitive construction, filled with various kinds of explosives and equipped with a simple pressure-type fuze. Because of their nonmetallic containers they could not be picked up by German mine detectors. Actually these mines had no greater effect than to damage or destroy the wheel which had run over them. Seldom did they cause any casualties among the drivers.

In the early stages of the campaign single vehicles were sometimes attacked by well-concealed Russian snipers. Even later, during their first fire raids on German convoys, the partisans usually remained out of sight. As their strength increased, they began to carry out regular attacks on highway traffic, using the same tactics as in their raids on railroad trains. The partisans would open surprise fire on a German motor convoy and then go over to a regular infantry attack which usually ended with the destruction of the vehicles, capture of the crews, and seizure of the supplies. In many cases the bodies of German soldiers who had belonged to the raided convoy were found later with all signs of having been brutally murdered by the partisans.

Bitter experience taught the Germans that the most dangerous roads were those that ran through impenetrable and often swampy forests, which by European standards were of gigantic size. It was practically impossible to advance into these woods for more than a mile or two, since anyone not familiar with the terrain would be left without a path and unable to find his bearings. Therefore, the Germans established a system of security strong points along all roads leading through partisan-infested areas. Single trucks were no longer permitted to pass through the forests. Depending on the degree of danger in each case, motor convoys of ten to thirty trucks with adequate crews and sufficient protection were formed and escorted through the partisan-infested woods from one control point to the next.

At the beginning of the Russian campaign the crews of German supply trucks had small arms, but no machine guns. Later on, after some truck convoys had been helplessly exposed to surprise fire and partisan raids, they were issued machine guns which were mounted on the platform of ½ to 1-ton trucks. At a still later stage of the campaign the trucks were lightly reinforced with armor plates. Shortage of personnel, however, precluded the use of special machine gun crews and placed an additional burden on the supply troops. On every trip the relief driver had to sit behind the machine gun, ready to fire, while the rest of the convoy personnel was constantly on the alert against surprise attacks. Soldiers returning from furlough were sometimes collected at security strong points along the roads and employed as escort personnel for supply convoys moving up to the front.

6. Attacks on Supply Depots

Now and then the partisans raided German supply dumps in army rear areas. But compared to other partisan incursions, such raids were quite infrequent, perhaps because these dumps and distributing points were usually located close to the front and therefore more strongly protected against surprise attacks.

The personnel in every supply installation, in addition to their regular work, were charged with interior guard duty and the protection against enemy attacks on the ground and from the air. A perimeter defense plan was drawn up for each installation. In case of attack prepared positions indicated in this outline were to be occupied and held by all personnel present at the installation. In most instances, however, the projected field fortifications could not be completed because of the pressure of time. A complex communications network consisting of radio, telephone, motorcycle messengers, and runners assured the rapid transmission of orders, reports, and calls for immediate assistance.

Russian air attacks on German supply installations showed a marked increase in 1942 and 1943. During the first winter of the campaign Russian air activity had been confined to isolated attacks by so-called "sewing machines"—obsolete aircraft with noisy engines—which dropped single, small-sized bombs and did little damage. But soon thereafter the Russians began to concentrate their air attacks on German supply lines on an ever increasing scale. Soviet air reconnaissance seemed to pay special attention to locating German supply installations; in contrast to the preceding period, even supply dumps close to the front were now subjected to frequent raids.

Wherever the supply troops used adequate precautions, these raids caused relatively little destruction. Major damage was prevented in most instances by maintaining proper safety intervals between stacks or burying supplies in the ground, as well as by the unhesitating commitment of all available personnel in case of emergency.

There was no evidence that the Russian civilians living in the immediate vicinity of these German supply dumps ever used their knowledge to pass information to the enemy, promote acts of sabotage, or facilitate partisan raids. While few of these advance supply installations were ever attacked by the partisans, it was established that in one particular area partisan convoys led by German-speaking individuals in German uniforms called for provisions, and by the presentation of the regular requisition forms they managed to obtain German supplies. This was made possible by the fact that the German forces were using almost exclusively Russian personnel for their socalled panje-convoys (columns of native horse carts), with only a few

Germans to supervise them. Thus it was relatively easy for the partisans to organize the same type of convoys without attracting undue attention and to disappear again as soon as their mission was accomplished.

German supply traffic on Russian inland waterways was seldom subjected to enemy interference; no instance is known in which the Russians mined their rivers. Wherever possible, river craft used for supply and transportation by the German forces were provided with makeshift armor and equipped with light guns.

SECTION IV

CONCLUSIONS

A. From the wealth of practical experience gained during the Russian campaign and particularly from the foregoing examples a number of important lessons can be derived.

1. The employment of peaceful means clearly offers the best assurance for military security in an occupied area. Failing that solution the only alternative lies in an all-out program of *active defense*.

2. In the selection and organization of security forces, despite the usual difficulties, the main emphasis must be placed on the high quality of personnel and equipment. No partisan-infested area can be cleared and rendered permanently safe by a force composed of old men who are equipped with foreign weapons and a few rounds of ammunition. If such security units fail to accomplish their mission, they are likely to become the laughing-stock of an inherently antagonistic population and their ineffective operations will have the result of strengthening the resistance of the enemy.

3. Anyone charged with responsibility for planning and conducting military operations must take into account the size, danger, and proper significance of the front behind the front. Any disruption of German rear communications anywhere in the vast expanse of occupied Russian territory was sure to have immediate effects which could be felt by virtually every German headquarters, indeed by every single unit. No similar experience had been made in any of the previous campaigns, with the possible exception of the Balkan operations. The full implications of this new problem became particularly obvious whenever the German armies in Russia were confronted with the perfect teamwork between the enemy behind their lines and the Russian forces in front. What happened in the rear area frequently served as a clue to the enemy's intentions at the front. It might be mentioned that German troops harbored no illusions about the nature of this added theater of operations. It did not take long until word was passed among the divisions on the line that the fighting against the partisans for the protection of rear communications was often more severe and resulted in larger numbers of casualties than actual combat at the front. Many a division brought to the rear for rehabilitation and there, as a sideline so to speak, employed in antipartisan operations, requested after a short time to be relieved of such duties and permitted to return to the front. This reaction alone should well support the contention that the front-behind-the-

front is a theater of operations in its own right. No longer is it appropriate to treat this zone as a stepchild or to regard it merely as the zone of communications in the traditional sense.

4. Any commander who is determined to conduct an *active defense* against partisan bands must of necessity accept the idea of committing regular combat forces in occasional mopping-up operations of partisan-infested areas. German experience during the Russian campaign clearly demonstrated that a passive defense based on scattered security strong points is not sufficient, no matter how well such a defense may be organized.*

5. The greatest promise of success lies in carrying the fight against partisans beyond the immediate vicinity of threatened supply lines and right up to the enemy's strongholds and rallying points. Careful reconnaissance is a paramount requirement for such operations. Without adequate knowledge of the terrain any expedition into a partisan-infested area can be no more than a plunge in the dark and will only lead to excessive losses in men and equipment. Another prerequisite is the current maintenance of accurate maps which cover the pockets of resistance and the assembly areas of partisan groups. Data for these maps can be obtained from local sources if the occupying troops are able to gain the confidence of the indigenous population.

6. Constant patrolling activity must be maintained not only on the main highways but also along the side roads. Occupied areas are to be kept under close surveillance at all times through a regular network of interlocking patrol posts. But even such patrols will only serve their purpose if at least some of their personnel are acquainted with the country and able to obtain information and reports from the local inhabitants. Therefore the careful selection and judicious employment of men who are familiar with the terrain, the language of the people, and the enemy's military tactics are among the principal prerequisites for the success of an active defense.

7. Commanders of village strong points or of local security units are to be granted complete authority for *local* antipartisan operations. This will enable them to take aggressive and successful measures immediately at the appearance of partisan bands, and obviate any lengthy and time-consuming inquiries or requests to higher headquarters. Small motorized forces must be available for the rapid pursuit of the enemy. Partisans operate at great speed; they appear on the scene, complete their mission, and withdraw again to their hideouts. Once they have disappeared into the woods, it is practically impossible to pick up their tracks.

---

*Ed.: See DA Pamphlet 20-230, *Russian Combat Methods in World War II*, pp. 107 ff.

8. Of equal importance is the constant use of aircraft for the surveillance of areas that are suspected or known to be infested by partisans. This is especially true of large forest regions. Wherever local terrain conditions render any ground reconnaissance impossible, it is only from the air that a rough estimate can be obtained of the whereabouts and activities of partisan forces.

9. It is clear, nevertheless, that there must be another solution to the entire problem of rear area security. In modern warfare even an active defense based on the combined efforts of combat troops and security forces cannot assure the complete elimination of partisan activities. In the area of Army Group Center, for instance, there were 80,000 to 100,000 partisans, who tied down a security force conservatively estimated at 100,000 men. The use of front-line divisions in mopping-up operations on a large scale—such as the combing of the Bryansk forest in the spring of 1943—had no more than a temporary effect; in no instance did the result of such operations justify their cost.

10. The only all-inclusive solution to the problem of rear area security seems to lie in the actual pacification of occupied enemy territory. In every country under military occupation there are people in all walks of life whose most ardent desire is the return to peace and normalcy, not to speak of those among them who for personal reasons are willing to support the policies of the occupying power. Cultivating their friendship, assuring them of one's peaceful intentions, and restoring the safety of their homes, their work, and their subsistence are the best guarantees for real security in the rear of the fighting troops.

11. News of good treatment travels just as fast as reports of bad treatment, and most people will decide quickly and intelligently what kind of treatment they prefer. Generally speaking, the civilian population in Russia was quite willing to cooperate. Moreover, the villagers themselves were ready to defend not only their homes but also their places of work against native plunderers, Red Army stragglers, and raiding partisans. The reopening of places of worship and the revival of long-neglected church services contributed greatly toward the establishment of good will.

12. Many other examples pointed to the wisdom of a policy of pacification. Although friendly and cooperative in the beginning, the inhabitants of some areas were soon driven into the arms of the partisans by improper treatment or unwise occupation policies. German military commanders or their troops were always the least to be blamed for such developments. But whenever an area was turned over to a German civilian administration, it did not take long until the attitude of the population changed from collaboration to hostility.

B. What then are the methods by which the indigenous population can be won over? What must be done to establish and maintain the security of rear areas?

1. The first and foremost prerequisite is the full confidence of the population in the good faith, as well as in the military capabilities of the troops fighting at the front or occupying the rear areas. Such confidence can be created by a sound, straightforward, and factual propaganda prepared and disseminated by individuals who are familiar with the Russian language, the population, and local living conditions. Extraneous ideas are to be avoided; whatever the people are told must be expressed in their own everyday language, on their own intellectual level, and concerned with their own immediate problems.

2. A thorough knowledge of Bolshevist doctrines and methods is indispensable, especially of those aspects which in the past have imposed hardships and suffering on the population. While being reminded of their unpleasant experiences, the people must be shown the road to freedom from Bolshevist oppression and communist ideology.

3. The Russian is a great believer in official papers. He is happiest when he has an official document, a stamped identification card, or an official pass in his hands. This propensity is to be cultivated, since it offers a fine medium of propaganda.

4. Typical Soviet propaganda methods, such as placards, bulletin boards, and oversize posters, should not be copied. If the Russian has little faith in Bolshevist propaganda, he will put even less in its imitation. He can be strongly influenced by pictures and statistical charts, provided that they are used to present clear and simple facts. At the same time an appeal to his emotions should be made in the wording and visual presentation of the propaganda material.

5. The Russian is not interested in pin-up girls. He wants to be told about western machinery, industrial operation, and farming; about the methods and profitableness of western private enterprise. He has toiled long enough for State and Party. Now he would like to know in what way and to what extent he may work for himself. In this respect he is looking for the help of the occupying power.

6. Propaganda, to be effective in Russia, must not operate with far distant goals, since Bolshevism presented the Soviet people with too many long-range promises in its Four Year Plans. The individual Russian wants to know:

> What will I get from the next harvest?
> May my children go to school?
> May they freely choose any vocation?

7. Russian youth want to have the right of choosing and freely practicing a profession. The Russian girl is not too domestically inclined; she is primarily interested in achieving an equal standing with men in all occupations.

8. Propaganda in occupied enemy territory must advocate measures which are practicable even in wartime and develop programs which can be put into operation prior to the termination of hostilities. The immediate aim must always be in the foreground; no more than a general outline should be given of the long-range goal.

9. The foremost propaganda agent is the individual member of the occupying forces, the man who is able to talk and associate with the Russians everywhere and to tell them what they want to know. At the same time he must have full authority to issue local regulations since it is well known that the Russian waits for directives, orders, and permits, rather than doing anything on his own. Convinced that it will harm him in the end, he avoids independent action wherever possible. But whatever he is ordered to do, he does willingly and wholeheartedly. This is an outgrowth of Russia's historical evolution under both czarist and communist rule, as well as an inherent national characteristic.

10. Speeches at public rallies or in meetings of municipal councils are an effective medium of propaganda. By far the best results are achieved wherever propaganda can be disseminated by word of mouth.

11. It goes without saying that the actions of the occupying forces must be in strict accordance with their propaganda. The start or resumption of work by the civilian population is to be ordered, but no forced labor must be permitted. Civilian food requirements are to be assured at a minimum subsistence level. Arbitrary actions by either the occupying power or the local administrative agencies are to be avoided under any circumstances. The resumption of work in native crafts and trades is to be given all possible aid and encouragement. Spiritual activities and religious freedom are to be restored by reopening the churches and protecting public worship.

12. Prisoners of war are to be well treated and used for productive work only. Wherever their presence is not needed and they are not likely to jeopardize the security of the occupying forces, they are to be released as soon as possible. Experience has shown that the early release of prisoners of war contributes greatly to the pacification of occupied territory.

13. Although as a general rule the free movement of civilians must be confined to their local communities, exceptions should be made to permit securing of food, attendance at public worship, and necessary travel in the event of illness.

14. The importance of work for everyone, with the assurance of adequate pay and subsistence, cannot be overemphasized. Unemployed and discontented masses of people, lacking the bare necessities and perhaps exposed to arbitrary acts at the hands of the occupying troops, represent an enormous danger to rear areas and communication lines. This is all the more true in the vast territory of Russia, where such dissatisfied elements are offered innumerable opportunities to disappear in forests and swamps, in the wilderness, and on river islands. Here nature provides fertile soil for the rapid growth of partisan bands.

☆ U.S. GOVERNMENT PRINTING OFFICE : 1984 O - 430-152

RAILROAD TRAFFIC DISRUPTIONS
IN THE
AREA OF ARMY GROUP CENTER
AUGUST 1943

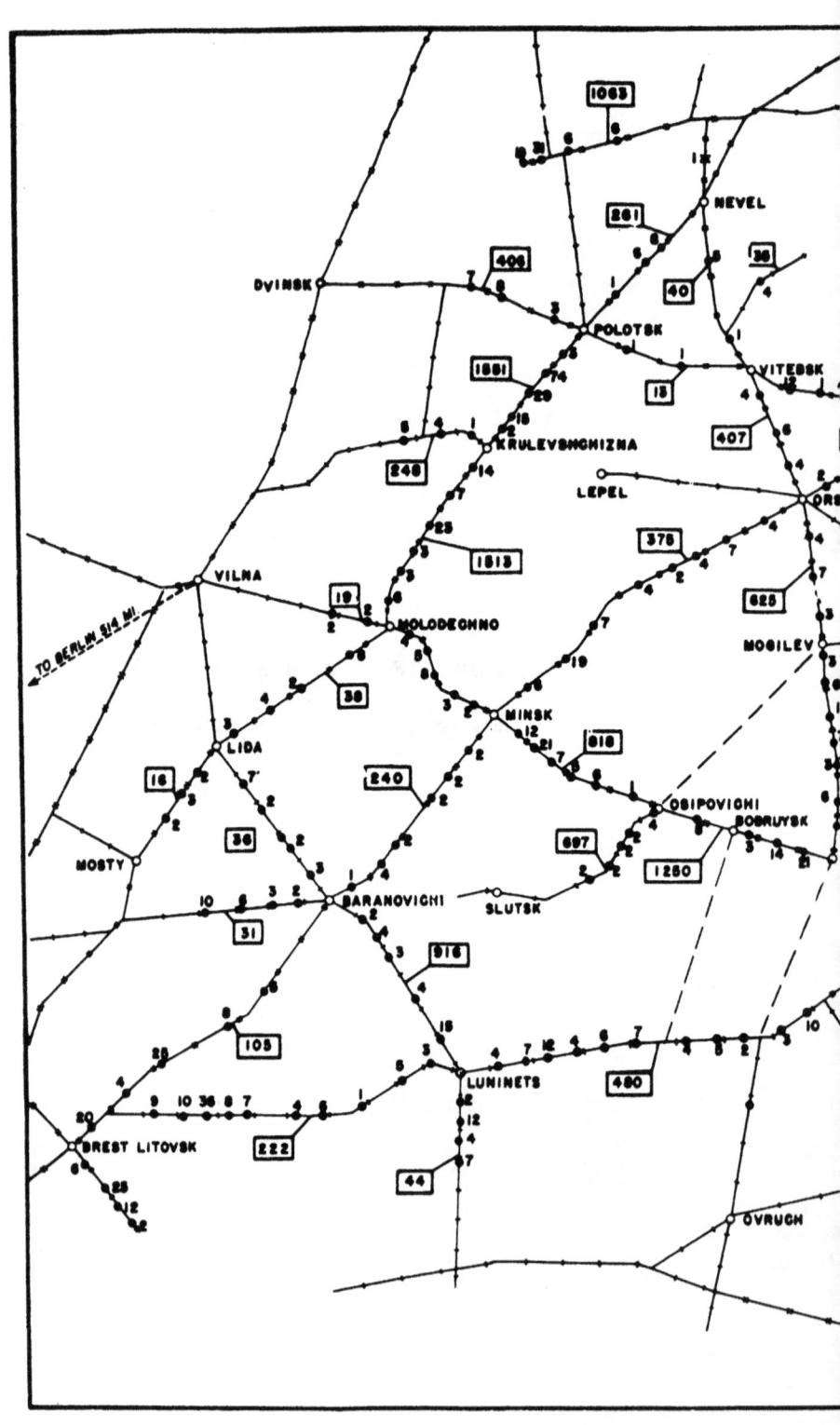

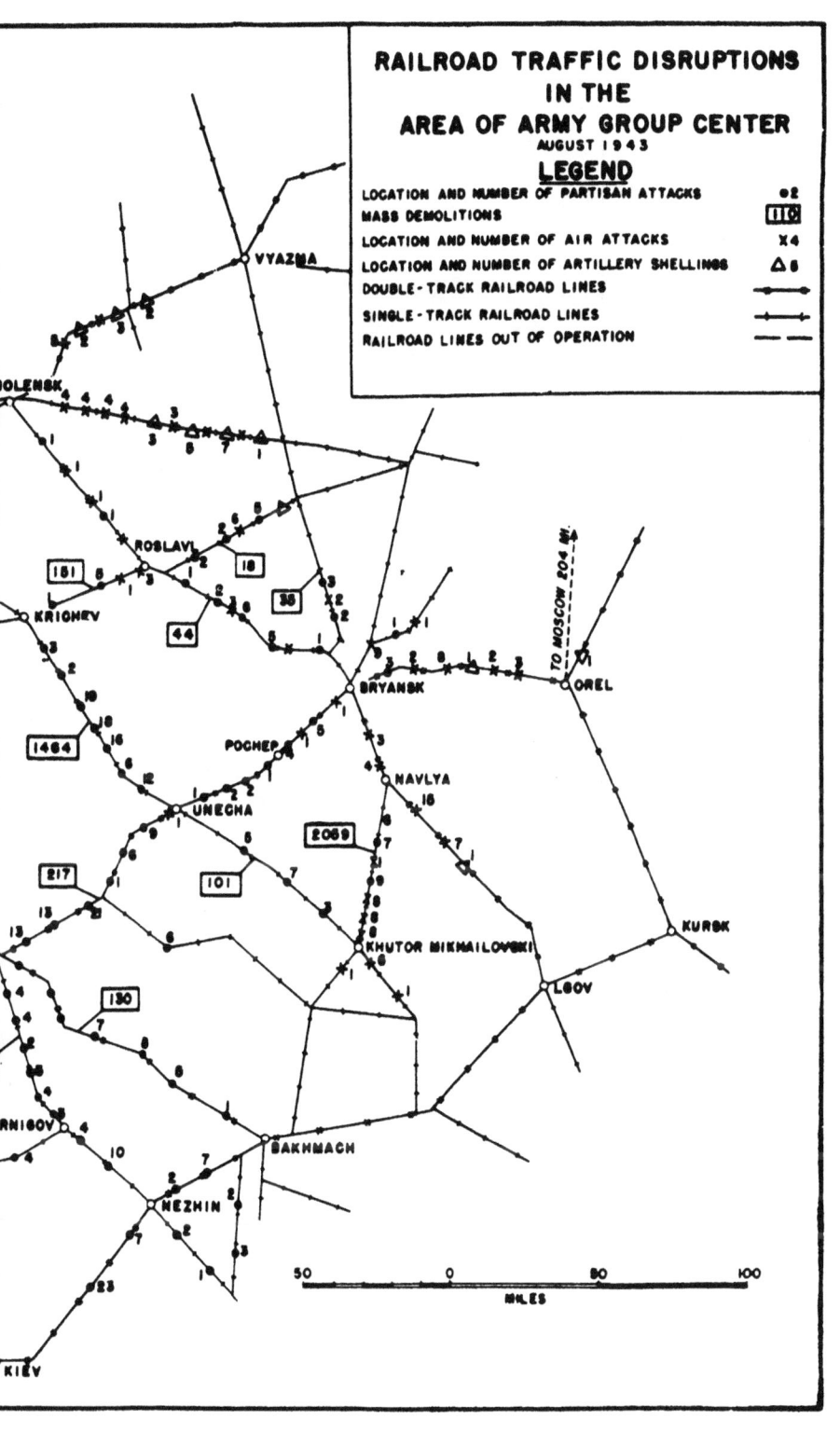

REFERENCE MAP
REAR AREA SECURITY IN THE EAST

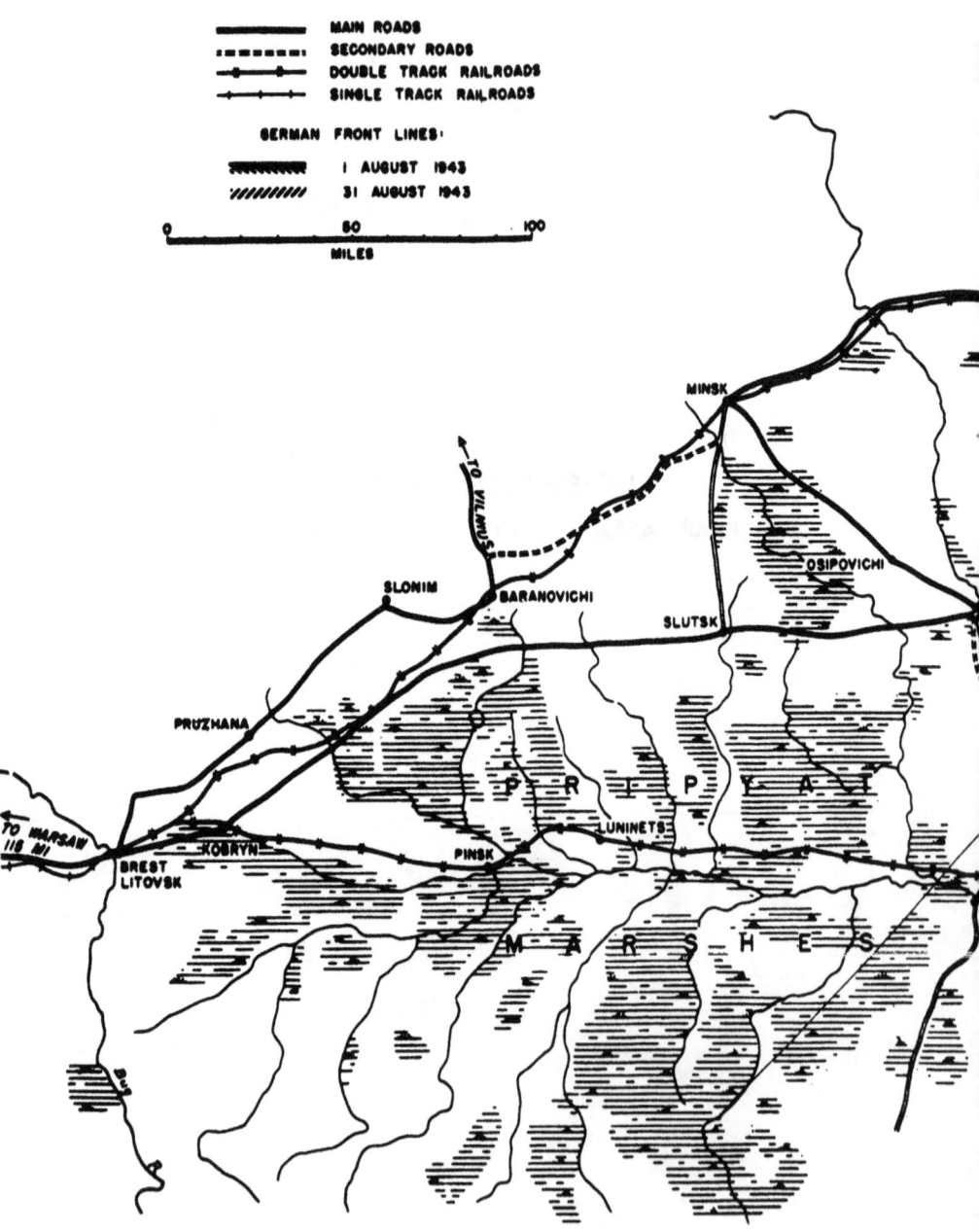

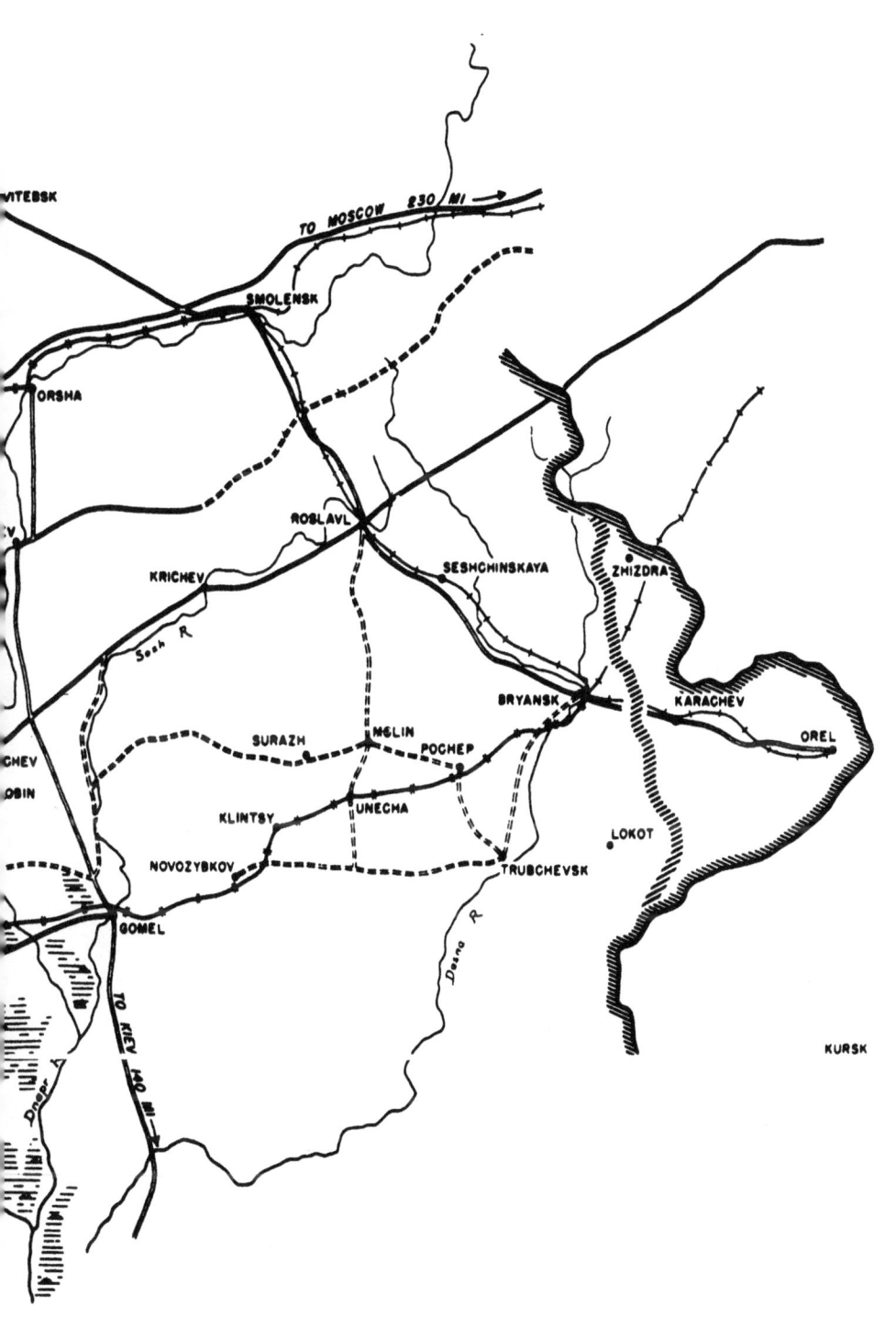

www.ingramcontent.com/pod-product-compliance
Lightning Source LLC
Chambersburg PA
CBHW061300040426
42444CB00010B/2437